GOLF
JOURNAL

THIS IS A 5.5 X 8.5 110 PAGE JOURNAL/DIARY TO USE AS YOU WISH.

100 PLUS LINED PAGES TO TAKE NOTES, WRITE STORIES, USE AS A DIARY OR WHATEVER YOU CAN THINK OF.

IT'S TIME TO HAVE FUN AND BE CREATIVE.

Dear Dad,   Dec'18

For all your Golfing Memoirs!

"hole in one"

"international
Golf tournament
winner".

love Sarah x.

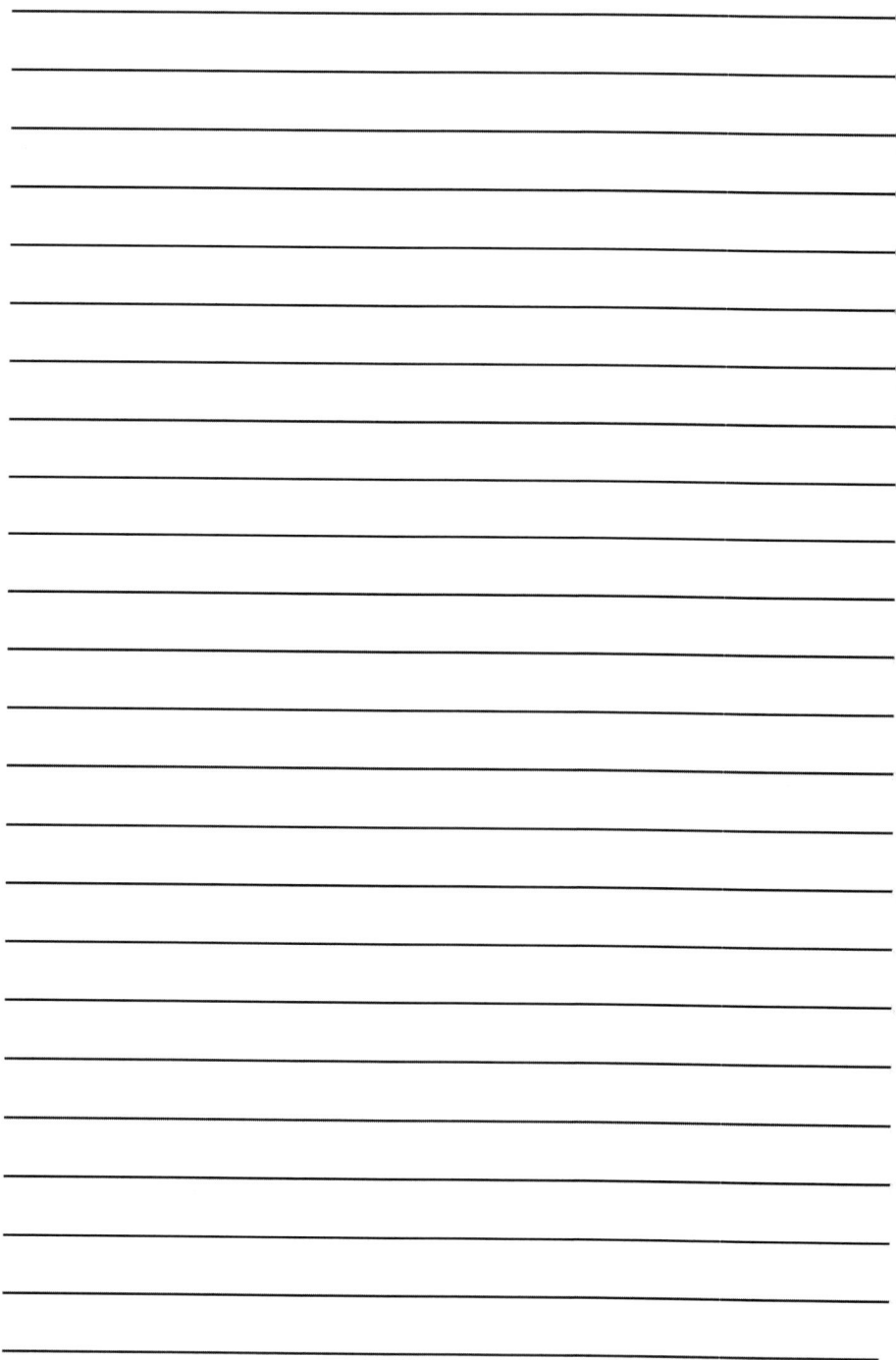

Do you have secrets you need to protect?

You may also be interested or know someone
who would enjoy our other journals

I Believe in Unicorns
I Believe in Bigfoot
I Believe in Angels
I Believe in Love
I Believe in Aliens
I Believe in Superheroes
I Believe in Dragons
My Own Joke Journal
Superhero Secrets

And Many More....

I HOPE YOU ENJOY THIS JOURNAL.

MANY MORE I BELIEVE JOURNALS
AND OTHER OPTIONS ARE AVAILABLE
AT:

niftyjournals.com

#WRITE
#CREATE
#ILLUSTRATE

THANK YOU FOR YOUR PURCHASE

38236487R00061

Printed in Great Britain
by Amazon